Second Home

Second Home

P O E M S

Randy Blasing

Copper Beech Press
Providence

Grateful acknowledgment is made to the editors of the magazines that first published certain of these poems: *The Carolina Quarterly*: "Cast-Iron Blimp"; *Michigan Quarterly Review*: "In a Word"; *The New Criterion*: "Toward an Anniversary"; *Poetry*: "Wishful Thinking," "Rock Country," "Daylight Saving," "Beside the Holy City's Sacred Pool," "Retriever"; *The Southern Review*: "Empire Builder," "Countdown," "The Boys"; *Southwest Review*: "Minor Ruin," "Home from Ionia"; and *The Yale Review*: "Second Home" (I, II, VII, XV, XVIII, XIX, XXV, XXVI, XXXVI).

Cover: *Old Çeşme*, by Ramo. Paraffin oil on paper, 25 x 33 cm. Photograph by Cesur Sert. Collection of Maria Laliberti Pagy. Used by permission.

Library of Congress Cataloging-in-Publication Data

Blasing, Randy.
    Second home / Randy Blasing.
    p. cm.
    ISBN 0-914278-79-7 (alk. paper)
    1. Sonnets, American. I. Title.

PS3552.L38 S43 2001
813'.54—dc21

                                                        2001017491

Set in Garamond by Louis Giardini
Printed and bound by McNaughton & Gunn
Manufactured in the United States of America
First Edition

for my son, John, & in memory
of my parents, Al & Mary

CONTENTS

Second Home

CHANGE OF LIFE

My friend the player vows he's written off
meaningless sex—i.e., sex without love—
but at a certain age all lovemaking
becomes an end in itself, not the means
to somebody's end, with no point beyond
the feeling of two souls conjoined to try
& give each other pleasure without end.

Since cutting to the payoff means letting
the future call the shots, as in the past,
the only way of staying in the present
moment remains to use the rhythm method
& draw out time by putting off the climax,
much as working the ins & outs of syntax
slows my progress toward the bottom line.

FIRST LOVE

I want to see you naked & your face
when you come—that's all I want to see said
about love anymore when desire threatens

it's run its course. Item: your dress made
of nubbled silk green as sea foam & as plush
to the touch as a pink-gold apricot

takes our decades together off my age
each time you wear it, as you must, with nothing
under its latticework of straps in back

& sheath fit with a slit up front. Its side
zipper allows, as now, both my hands easy
access to the sunless globes of your T

& A, which I have brought to light. They feel
exactly as my ten fingers remember.

CALL LETTERS

After my father died, my mother fell
asleep to voices on the radio,

her black-&-gold Emerson portable
talking her into letting the day go

each night. WCCO-AM
had her ear, & its soothing idle chatter

had the last word. Up late, I find you've dropped
off to the music of the silver blaster

inherited from her. A year older
than my heartbreaker father got to be,

I've stopped living him down, dead to you now,
& started listening to my heart's cry

for love as to the songs on PRO-
FM that rock my own half-empty bed.

DO YOU READ ME?

The clock was ticking as the oldies spun
into the night another Saturday,
& you were shocked that I would ever try
getting on the map by phoning the DJ
to call the tune myself. When I requested
"Walking Home from School with You," he asked
the artist's name, which I had been unable
to recollect since I slipped 45's
on the turntable of my blond Magnavox
circa 1958, but that instant
"Chuck Mabry" came to me from forty years
away in a heartbeat, my memory traveling
involuntarily at the speed of light.

He dropped off the charts about 1960,
I was told, & most likely wouldn't be
around the studio, but if his records
remained on file, I'd hear from him, for sure.
You begged me not to use my name, for fear
the world would learn I didn't have a life
& wallowed in the past, lost in nostalgia.
Except my name means nothing, & whoever
found me pathetic had to be, it figured,
in the same boat by reason of their listening
& dreaming of what might have been back when,
the future proven non-negotiable.
You'll find me here next week, same time, same station.

IN A WORD

Poetry is really a form of worship.
Robert Hayden

Sunday my neighborhood church rang a bell
as if for me, but I turned a deaf ear,
islanded as I was by boxy Stanzas,
Isuzu Styluses, & Mercury
Tracers. Soon my Accord flew me beyond
where the last freeway, like railroad tracks run
into the ground, ran out of gas in weeds.

Landing in the cratered parking lot
of an abandoned dog track, I got down
on my knees before the white elephants
displayed like holy relics at a swap meet
vaster than any rummage sale that Nana
could have imagined mounting in the basement
of St. Olaf's. I retrieved her red-&-white-

handled bread knife she used on loaves she'd baked
from flour stored in the wine-red bin beneath
her apron-white counters, next to the cupboard
where I stashed my green wood-&-cast-iron
flatbed I didn't want to lose when moved
into a new house at seven. My first
brass-buttoned Rawlings glove my dad gave me

for Easter came to light, plus his shotgun
(in its tan leather case) he kept well-oiled
deep in the farthest reaches of his closet,
& even the linen print Grandpa brought
my mom home from Mexico reappeared
out of nowhere, its sombrero'd Rip Van
Winkle there under his saguaro. The world

I'd known back at my feet, I lost track of time
among its findings, but what I found missing
& gone for good was my child's faith in prayer—
unless this mumbling to myself I do,
not from or by the Book but in a book,
amounts to worshiping a greater power
that promises a future for the past.

CAST-IRON BLIMP

Is it related to a lead balloon,
this silver Tootsietoy of heavy metal
fashioned like a zeppelin Collectibles
Unlimited wheels out & floats for upwards
of a song? Anchored by its sky-high price,

it still gives rise to my construing, al-
chemist of memory I aspire to be,
my father's dwelling on the *Hindenburg's*
going down in flames as his private image
of truth: enterprises fueled by hot air

were fated to crash & burn. My small business
has been not to forget his word was gold
since I went underground & first sat down
at his weighty gilt-lettered Underwood,
holding my breath to see what words would fly.

AMERICAN FLYER

As I step forward into history,
Narragansett Flea shows me where the years went,

& childhood things I thought I'd put away
& lost for good turn up, materialized

before my eyes but mint & out of sight
as far as cost. My smoke- & whistle-blowing

American Flyer train advertised
in black & white conjures my parents' ghosts:

my mother in an apron & my father,
gone prematurely gray at Okinawa,

stayed up all Xmas Eve when I was seven,
landscaping tracks with shavings glued to plywood

& painted the same shade as their dream lawn.
Once more my Great Northern engine parades

its peach refrigerator, lemon boxcar,
& rust caboose past the façade of stores

they jigsawed me. I can still see their sign
for "Green Wall Drug," their little play on *Walgreen*

the touch, they let me feel, that made their day
& set me on the track of words, in time.

EMPIRE BUILDER

Trains have carried me away ever since
my mother's mother scolded her (I heard)
in Minneapolis, because she stepped
off the Hiawatha from Chicago

pregnant with me while the Forty-Niner aimed
to ship my just-commissioned father west
of the Golden Gate into the Rising Sun.
Transported by the hoot the Minuteman gives

shooting through Providence again tonight,
I backtrack to the eight-year-old I was,
burning my fingers on the silver rails
nearly molten in the August heat

as I sacrificed my blackest copperhead
to the tanked-up Empire Builder that would pass
below my Golden Valley ranch with cargo,
under wraps, targeted for the Far East.

Fifteen years down the line, my hands were tied
the April afternoon I couldn't look
when a green train bursting with greener kids
bound for the jungle screamed through my backyard

outside Richmond. When I left home the fall
before & rode the last Orient Express
from Paris to its end in Asia Minor,
I never dreamed I'd starve till past Trieste.

A guest worker escaping Munich wanted
my blue Parker fountain pen for his bread
but didn't know I meant to live by ink,
hungry to swallow the world whole like this.

SECOND HOME

for Mutlu

I
Duty-free Hermes in my pocket now,
your Joy postponed again, Memorial Day
I'm back mixing spirits with Blondie soda.
Each lemon-lettered bottle is the green
of an Astroturf mini soccer field
fenced in on the scorched earth between a mosque
—"*Allah* in Xmas lights!"—& cinder blocks
by law a house if crowned with the trademark
corrugated Eternity-brand roof
against the elements. (Once four in number,
they were themselves the building blocks, as per
local lore.) Meanwhile, Izmir has named
its new airport after a glamourboy
prime minister folks hated to see hanged.

II
Your father's house he bought with precious metal
on his deathbed is ancient history,
undermined by a high-rise boom & paper
bills all colors. On the five, emerald-cloaked
Rumi yields to the thick-waisted hourglass
of a sepia cooling tower, time changed
from a grain-by-grain trickle to a landslide
& family plots to story upon story.
Even as I write, F-16s crackle
like thunder off the balcony the powers-
that-be dictate the narrow limits of.
The lightning is day breaking on the cart
a turbaned milkman's decked with thumbnail landscapes,
his white nag rainbowed with pom-poms & tassels.

III
Low-bridged by a doorway on *9 September,*
the ferry crossing to "The Other Side,"
I stagger for a moment with my burden
after I've duly sacrificed a coin
to the cold gatekeeper & slipped my wafer
between its iron lips to pass from here,
my pockets empty but my hands full
of such provisions as Ayvalik olives
pink as my neighbor's birthmarked face, roast almonds
from Knidos, dried Malatya apricots.
The evening air as thick with this day's smoke
as the landing is with souls at their day's end,
I try walking in the shoes of my friend
Murat, dead at my age on the Cyprus boat.

IV
Sailing home on the ferry from the old
gold market, we sat beside—his card read—
"Mr. Charly" *(sic)*. He asked me point-blank
what it felt like being a citizen
of the country that the whole world has in mind,
the way at lunch *USA* was tattooed
in lime & lemon close to the hearts of both
the pizza-thrower & his boy Friday.
We'd come from where our seatmate was a jeweler,
& coincidence refreshed my memory
of how events are riddled with connections,
just as gold was the thread that tied our lives
together, wound around my finger like string
that once returned me constantly to you.

V

No sooner had you gotten off the trolley
to catch the cross-bay ferry you took home
from school as a girl not twelve, & walked back
alone from the boat station to your house,
than all the neighborhood kids greeted you
with news your father had just died at last.
The minute that you opened the front door
& found your mother & your grandmother
waiting in the living room, your father
in the next, you closed the door on the past
& lost yourself in English, which he'd hoped
would see you through the future he foresaw.
These forty years no memories have surfaced
from those eleven years with him you buried.

VI

At last your stepfather turned grief to grievance.
Among the first wave of UN troops sent
to Korea forty-plus years ago,
he saw one in three of his countrymen
sacrificed—half of them in four days
when, covering the U.S. Marines' retreat
at Chosin Basin, they fought Red Chinese
to the death. A MASH doctor, he couldn't eat
finely chopped Chinese food without recalling
his young patients cut to pieces. One year
at fifteen bucks a month cost him his hair
& earned him a lifetime supply of nightmares,
despite ice cream delivered to the front
or R&R in MacArthur's Japan.

VII

Humming the Marines' hymn still gives me gooseflesh.
My boy won't hear of it & sings a Turkish
anthem about Gallipoli, where one
among my Welsh grandfather's fourteen siblings
(James), shot on horseback in a custom-printed
postcard from the front, fought a losing battle.
Artichokes are bristly thistles whose heads
were meant to roll, I see from someone's field.
Marched to the sea, my son drops his M-16
facsimile near a Greek War redoubt,
his future a question mark; thyme, still green,
goes to my head. I aim to freeze the scene
the way jam preserves in amber the scent
of last summer's peaches, flushed & inflamed.

VIII

My kid missed his carotid artery
by a hair last night, slipping off a wall
on a stake that shored up an oleander.
The night before, I'd seen him lying flat
on his back in a dream—dead to the world,
to all appearances—& thought the worst.
I found him hollering, an arrow lodged
deep in his throat, & plunged into the dark
for a medicine man. Going back six years,
the second he was born I saw in him
my father, who nearly stabbed his jugular
when he tripped running downhill with a knife
at six. His mother bore him to a doctor,
who stitched him up. His life hung by a thread.

IX

Green crosses earmark this holiday's victims
huddled like a team of all followers,
putting their heads together to no purpose.
Their flesh haggled over & sold for X
number of pink & orange bills, the shepherds
give them each a last pat on the back,
rope them into car trunks, & slam the lids
on them, hostages sans blindfolds & duct tape.
My black-eyed, -eared, & -nosed white lamb, with patches
of *café-au-lait* & polka-dotted shins,
gets his throat slit in Allah's name tomorrow,
sacrificed so that I can thank the gods
my son survived an accident in his blood,
the nick in his neck Artemis's mark.

X

The blades the town's itinerant knife-sharpener
honed finely yesterday have done their work.
The thin man hunched over his collapsible
four-legged stand in the shade kept his nose
to the grindstone he set spinning when he tapped
his right foot, as if marking time to music
he alone heard. Each hysterical victim,
first blindfolded with a white muslin scarf
used to cover a woman's hair in mosques,
was slashed from ear to ear to please a higher
power worshiped by spilling blood for real
(the gauze-like cloth stained red indelibly).
This morning I still feel the heat beneath
the olive where my animal's strung up.

XI

The butcher takes the head (the brains & tongue
delicacies), the tail for tallow, & hooves
for gelatin. The snaky entrails get
unceremoniously buried, nothing
beyond a hole beneath the reach of dogs.
An Air Force tractor gathers up the skins
to keep the butts of Phantom fighter pilots
toasty at unfathomable altitudes
when they go dueling with the Greeks' Mirages.
The still-warm flesh lies quivering in pans.
We'll eat the lion's share of meat; the rest
will feed the poor, nightwatchmen & their kin
who sacrifice their days that I may sleep
in peace, dreaming A-bombs on CNN.

XII

All smiles & green eyes, the watchman who fled
the Kurdish bloodbath in the east by running
off with a smuggler's daughter once went out
on someone's limb & shook down mulberries
for me; I came home bloodstained as a butcher.
Then things slowly disappeared from our place:
a single hand towel, a favorite sweater,
an emerald Volvo & a ruby Saab
from our boy's collection of Hot Wheels, a rug.
When the cops tried returning to their rightful
owners some stolen goods found in the cave
where his wife had caught him with her best friend,
the mullahs called our missing rug their mosque's,
but he confessed he'd lifted it from us.

XIII

Having passed the last of the holy days,
the smell of blood impossible to wash
off my hands, I start in harvesting thyme
to season the thighbone I'll burn to Zeus
—in other words, the skewered flesh I'll charcoal
for ourselves—once the weather turns around.
When the wind is right, it brings home our wrongs:
in each cove, black & white plastic bags do
a dead man's float, the yarrow-leaf-green water
clotted with tar drops like India ink
I always spattered from my pen in Art.
Before I go the way of the sea's fish,
I give my word I hold the days themselves
sacred, & clouds unfold their silver linings.

XIV

When our unsmiling Kurdish postmaster
fixed his wolf eyes on me as if he'd seen
death itself step into his marble office,
he knew I'd ask to give wings to my words
& he would have to locate what it cost
somewhere inside this morning's fat printout
he cracked as if it surely hid a bomb,
because the postal rates had changed on him
overnight. But he warmed up when he saw
(& rubber-stamped) the postcard I would send
to show my tribe's last remaining members
a white sheep & a black, with flowery peasants.
The mountains in the background were his home
where, his stature argued, he'd be a chief.

XV
A Black Sea village girl of five, your mother
glimpsed herself squished upside down in a round
mirror small as a pocket watch—no doubt
the only looking glass at home—inlaid
below the latch of the hope chest she'd sprawled
across & recollected suddenly,
thanks to the one I had just bargained for:
green & decorated with Trees of Life
(charcoal branches of pear-shaped saffron flowers).
She'd wondered, she recalled some sixty years
later, if she could crawl inside & find
herself. By opening in memory
that box roughly the size of a child's coffin,
she met the face behind her face at last.

XVI
On his red bike my boy shows me myself
on mine at the same age, but training wheels
have given him the hand my father lent
to me, going in circles in the yard.
When I finally straightened out, resisting
gravity's pull with my balancing act,
I shot across the lawn toward the street
my mother, raising her head from her nonstop
sewing, reminded me had been dug up.
Unmindful of her last words, I went sailing
off the deep end. I still can't keep my feet
on the ground, driven to unwitting flights
like this. My son flies down the road, his face
now my mother's bent over her machine.

XVII
Caught in a long line of slow-moving traffic,
I cursed my fate till I stuck out my neck
& learned why I was crawling—a wood coffin
a host of men carried on their shoulders
like a sedan chair, ferrying their hero
the length of the town. Like a green wave cresting
above them, an emerald cloth inscribed with gilt
Arabic script shrouded his box, head pointed
like a boat's prow above the wider body
that narrowed to a squared-off stern. Our green
grocer in the crowd whispered that the man
was only thirty, which explained the mourners:
grief was written all over their young faces,
the lines starting to engrave themselves there.

XVIII
I tell the watchman at Erythrae we met
seven years ago when, unknown to me,
my son here got a foothold in his mother.
He shows me what they add up to for him—
no teeth in half his mouth. The Byzantines,
says the cross of a new TV antenna
springing from his ruin, have the last word.
Green thumbs of almonds, downturned, nix the Romans.
Artichokes, gone to seed, sprout tufts as purple
as urchins in the sea that brought Greeks from Troy.
Above it all, mock dogfights buzz like static.
Among the shards of earthenware my son
collects, a snake hacked in two stops me cold:
time, that great leveler, will cut me short.

XIX
In the sanitarium at Pergamum
the *S*-shaped snakes carved in stone hiss in English.
You thought they looked more than a little phallic
when I spied a postcard of an oil lamp
(Roman) in the museum, which depicted
a man taking a woman from behind.
While he reclined, she writhed & put the back
of a hand to her brow, beside herself.
I searched high & low for the pedestals
inscribed to Homer, Sappho, & the guy
who invented parchment. The child I was
discovered it in Philadelphia
in a browning Declaration. The world turns,
it said, on how we represent ourselves.

XX
She says to come closer so I can measure
the swelling in her cheek from her bad tooth.
With my bad eyes I can't get close enough
& only shake my head in sympathy.
Word has it in her time she moonlighted
as a lady of the evening. Now she's kept
on a short leash by a husband she supports
as a cleaning woman. Still, she cleaned house
next door while entertaining somebody
she faked not seeing follow her to work
the other day. This morning she inquires
if I will take her picture, & reclines
on the shaken green kilim I'm preserving
in a snapshot. She smiles with her lips sealed.

XXI
Taken to America as a kid,
my shrink friend lost his mother at the age
of seven to a cause that he still finds
mysterious. But he can totally
recall his visiting Niagara Falls
& driving through Sequoia's giant redwood
complete with its convenience store inside.
Or is he just remembering the slides
shot at the time, before he came back home
& his father drowned in Ephesus's pool?
Orphaned at nine, he has made himself up
this way, asking whether he's dreaming something
or recollecting it. For his purposes,
I remind him, if it feels true, it is.

XXII
Like someone hiding from the ozone hole
today, my father steered clear of the sun,
light-skinned as he was, but he'd have liked
how boiled sweet corn comes to the beach, gold
as the pupil of a "day's-eye," anointed
with kosher salt, & wrapped back in its husks
like hot tamales. In his youth he worked
summers canning niblets for Green Giant.
"Shoepeg" remained his lifelong favorite,
the pearly kernels packed in silver tins
—dwarfish themselves & marked with fleurs-de-lys—
I watched my mother buy at the Red Owl.
I see his neck sunburned, summer & winter,
by Fleischmann's sour corn mash—bronzed white lightning.

XXIII

As careful as if he were stacking eggs,
the melon man piles his wheelbarrow high
with lemon-yellow casabas striped lime.
Though he's sitting on a gold mine, he's proud
to say land isn't something a man sells.
No shoes on his feet, no plumbing at home,
his clothing only a patchwork of rags,
he's made his lone concession to the world
a shortwave for reaching his sons long gone
to sea. I called on him at sundown once,
but his wife sighed he had already drowned
in the bottle I had smuggled him before.
Asked why he drinks, he cried he's sick of living!
It's true: he'd sooner die than modernize.

XXIV

If, like my mother, I should die alone
after tucking myself into my own bed,
the last thing I will see will be the kilim
I'm using as a bedspread that was woven
by some poor girl in Anatolia
early this century, who added a new
wrinkle to a pattern, centuries old,
of linked red lozenges dazzling as stars:
three shades of blue (lapis, turquoise, powder),
combined with two of green (almond & olive),
all run together in waves the color
she only dreamed about & I could hold
my breath forever spying on below
the sea's deep-navy cover off the coast.

XXV

Seyyid gives me his word I take him at
that his shop's kilims are as soft as silk,
all natural, old, & indestructible.
Just as the truth lies somewhere in between
his claims & my suspicions, we arrive
together at the final cost by splitting
the difference between the fortune that he asks
& the pittance I first offer in return.
I feign indifference to the piece I crave;
acting, too, he complains he'll sacrifice
his profit. In the end I pay the price
I can afford, while he gets what he needs.
Such back-&-forth weaves the social fabric.
In fact, "shopping" translates as "give-&-take."

XXVI

On Sunday yet it fell into my hands,
a Koran handwritten three hundred years
before & sold to me without profit
by Muslim law, which also says it mustn't
ever sink below my bellybutton.
The scribe who copied out its words repeated
the Prophet's deed of taking down God's word
by dictation. Blood-red, a drop of ink
punctuates each couplet. Lulling my will
asleep—losing myself in counting beats
per measure—& submitting to the law
of numbers, I inscribe what comes to mind
out of nowhere, as it seems, much the way
the lines before me now originated.

XXVII

Under the Marshall Plan, Kazim the agri-
culturalist uprooted Reds from Rhode
Island, which rule the roost in Turkey now.
As a boy he learned German from his father,
an officer times made the Kaiser's ally,
then taught himself English & the Persian
I hear when he recites Omar Khayyam.
Cultivating the roots of words, he argues
Allah arises from Egyptian's *ox*,
sacred for the shot in the arm it gave
crops with its droppings when it plowed a furrow.
Its hieroglyph, turned on its head, reads *alpha*
in Greek & *A* in Latin. What he's not
saying, I am: the alphabet is God.

XXVIII

My son's playmate down the block spoke Ladino
at home & with an accent on the street
because his people were Sephardic Jews,
who'd landed here five hundred years ago
(escaping with their lives & their religion
the Inquisition) & lived happily
thereafter. They passed on their foreign language
to tell them where they'd come from—in a word,
what they believed & who they were from first
to last. His mother & his uncle knew
perfect English, which reminded me
Columbus had left Spain at the same time
but in the opposite direction. Learning
his friend's Turkish, my son thus closed the circle.

XXIX

When I stepped out of Turkey's shipping lines
after booking passage to the Greek island
opposite where Homer was born, the town
fell quiet in the wake of a small craft
built for one that, flat-bottomed, bobbed again
as wave on wave in a sea of hushed men
launched a featherweight upon the waters
via the mosque. The day before, tradition
had set the poor soul's worn brogues outside his door
for whoever needed them to cross over
to spring from fall & winter, when the weather
calls for leather in any shape or form.
Picking up where the dead's black shoes left off
keeps me standing on my own cold feet.

XXX

Asked, JM warned me about the allure
of local color I had to get past,
he said, to access my own past abroad.
But how blind myself to an octopus
my newborn's mauve in '86, its eyes
the amber of the fog lights on my father's
maroon '46 Zephyr; to the finger-
long red mullets a boy from Black Point called
"yellow pants" after the gold stripes running
down their sides as along the seams of Andy
Frain ushers' fancy pants in '56;
or to the double kilim ('76)
dyed teal with the skin of green pistachios
I tasted landing here in '66.

XXXI

My father, at the age I turned today,
was lying on his back with his hands tied,
forbidden to lift a finger. Heartbroken,
he needed me to shave him, who had fought
three years in the Pacific & foresaw
my generation (I'd just started shaving)
going back & finishing up in Asia.
On the black-&-white, hyped-up JFK
promised us the world. Frost toed the line,
blinded by the moment, then turned to memory.
The President, the poet, & my father
were gone in three years, but LBJ tried
shanghaiing me to Vietnam, whose shadow
reaches across continents to this day.

XXXII

I'd hardly come to a full stop in Konya
when a guy started pitching me a kilim
& I heard music drifting from a flute.
Rumi's tomb smelled like a gymnasium
from tourists' marching through in sweaty socks
as if inside a mosque. Lightning jumped
between a bearded merchant & a woman
revealing just eyes & ankles. Dating back
ten centuries, before the Ottomans
prevailed & outlawed representing humans,
Seljuk ceramics in the dim museum
you dug up there featured your button nose,
fine lips, & coffee eyes wide-set like Jackie's
that bought & sold me all those years ago.

XXXIII
Evening in Cappadocia. A shepherd
leading his flock to water to the tune
of his flute wore his woolen sports jacket
draped over his shoulders à la Marcello
Mastroianni in *La Dolce Vita*.
His lambs drank peacefully from the same stone
oasis of a spring that satisfied
my own thirst not a minute earlier.
I saw the sun burn down to nothing more
than one red coal small as his cigarette
glowing in the night that slowly welled up.
Darkness closed the book on another day,
his sheep folded between plain brown wrappers.
His flute calls the tune of that chapter still.

XXXIV
First, the Greek sister in a habit nodded
across the lake-sized gulf & spat out, "Turkey!"
Then she unveiled the 1822 bones
of the 25,000 Greeks on Chios
memorialized in verses by Lord Byron
—she showed me his handwriting on the wall—
& mourned each Easter there for getting burned
in church by Turks, who'd lost (she failed to mention)
as many Muslims to firebrands from Samos.
I wish that both parties worshiped their common
mother, sea-blue earth, not their different fathers
indifferent in heaven. At the Pearly Gates
they'll ask our mothers' names, because we know
for certain only who our mothers are.

XXXV

One long-gone summer in Bodrum, Greek jets
from Cos would strafe the town at dawn, according
to Turkish spies in Athens where the junta
had met all night to widen Cyprus fighting.
We jumped from bed & hit the mobbed dark streets,
my mouth dry as the creeks here in July.
I saw us in a black-&-white newsreel
of history's innocent victims gunned down
by diving Stukas. Your half-brother stumbled
along with us, his knees knocking at twelve.
Suddenly I felt twelve again myself,
a Little Leaguer watching beetle-browed
Mike Hall quake the same way when he led off
at Skippy Field back in prehistory.

XXXVI

Bias, the first autobiographer,
came from here, as did the first woman
architect, Phile, who designed the city's
reservoir that survives in principle
as the spring-fed pool at its watering hole
some drunk tourist is always diving into.
I raise my son to occupy the throne-
like stone seat reserved for whoever climbs
to the theater, no once-in-a-lifetime
ascent to Alexander-proof Termessus
but a trip to the top of the then known world
I've taken four straight decades. In the spirit
of Priene's native son so aptly named,
I slant my history toward myself.

XXXVII
You who collect seashells on every beach
gathered them in Miletus, where the sand
that, silting up the harbor over time,
left it high & dry & buried the marble
columns paving the way to Didyma.
Once a year the holy flocked there to pay
Apollo homage & get their fortunes told
by a sacred source. Walking in their shadow,
we knew their future who had read their past
& shared, if not their faith in a wellspring
of voices, their fate your shells made concrete.
We took the road destined in the end
for oblivion, leaving in our day
Thales Café for Hotel Oracle.

XXXVIII
When we first visited Apollo's temple
at Didyma, unearthed for us by Fraser
& Stella on their trip around the world,
I knelt & heard the oracle confirm
with silence that the past could tell me nothing.
Here we found sanctuary from the war
on Cyprus three years later, our motel
the one still open on the blacked-out coast,
& eight years afterward showed Mike & Karen
the hole in the stones. Then last night our son,
hugging his pyrographic backgammon set,
followed the same road. Retracing our path,
ear to the ground again, I hear these steps
tap out my future when it's in the past.

XXXIX
I'd flown to Bird Island when my mother
landed at Izmir's old air-base airport
with no one meeting her & wept alone
on your doorstep, reported neighbors, shaking
their heads at how her son could let the woman
find herself a room in a foreign city.
She never even mentioned my snafu.
At heart I couldn't share my reverie
of summer in the holy land I'd found.
Worse, I felt embarrassed when each new sight
only resembled what she'd seen at home.
In twenty years I've come to realize
I follow in her footsteps everywhere,
linking my days with correspondences.

XL
Her firebombed temple coin-bright silver pools,
I stand in awe of blissed-out Artemis
of Ephesus again. At first I figured
she was all alabaster breasts, except
they had no nipples, & on second thought
I saw her honeycombed with eggs, unless
this patron saint of virgins wouldn't make
an emblem of fertility. In fact,
she's hung with testes representing bulls
castrated in her honor like the priests
unmanned by their own hands to serve Diana,
together with her earliest incarnation
as Cybele. Each new initiate
ran howling through the streets & flung his bloody

XLI

organs through an open door at random;
the lucky household owed their former owner
food & clothes for life. No Medusa
freezing me with a look at Didyma,
she shares the Buddha's *Mona Lisa* smile
fixed in marble, as if inviting all
such meanings as she is invested with
—goddess, mother, virgin, slut, & witch.
My mother, Mary, had the wrong idea
about you when she sold you on not buying
a white dress for our wedding but a gold
you could recycle some less august day,
only to show up wearing white herself.
The Virgin Mother lies not far from here.

XLII

While I sat scribbling in my room as always
the morning of our wedding on this day,
you tangled with the beauty operator
Mary, who'd turned your head into a beehive.
The week before, Helen in your office cried
at Tonkin Gulf, a Cassandra in her way;
torched on-screen, Watts previewed decades. At night
the Beatles, not the Twins, played at the stadium,
& at Cape Kennedy Apollo 5
shot for the moon. When guests showed us the door,
we stepped—half-blind—into the dark future
everyone but us knew would see us hit
earth-shaking thunder & sky-splitting lightning,
found here in August once in a lifetime.

XLIII
There I stood in some astronaut's ex-pad
in the east Eighties, twenty-five stories
closer to the moon than the man on the street,
& talked long-distance to my eighth-grade friend
about our common flame of two decades
ago. Sometimes I still dance cheek-to-cheek
with her to "Earth Angel" down his basement,
her pointy little breasts under her crimson
sweater tickling my ribs, et cetera,
& I still see him walking out the door
to Enga's Funeral Home with a blue suit
for my father, whom he'd trusted to inform
a scoutmaster had gotten friendly with him
inside a tent. Speaking from Chicago,

XLIV
where I last saw him over a six-pack
of Falstaff's the night before he moved out
to Vietnam, he couldn't tell his mother
wrote him off behind his back a confirmed
bachelor & a "dyed-in-the-wool"—her words—
Republican. His father turned up bombed,
a specialist from Ithaca in feed,
& volunteered the phrase "American
civilization" was a contradiction
in terms. The scene flashed back to me tonight
like a streaking meteor when I sat down
to nose around among the stars & play
connect-the-dots with ancient constellations,
the way I fill in the blanks of the past.

XLV

The sea a lake of blue smoke, the wind holds
its fire. My olive doesn't move a muscle.
Last wisps of fog drift inland & dissolve
like clouds of dust. I leave my fading trace
upon the water stroke by stroke, a finger
writing on a steamed-up mirror. Backstroking
underwater, a swimmer camouflaged
the turquoise of the depths flexes her hips
for all the world but stays within herself,
never breaking the surface of her dream.
First thing today, I bought six "yellow-ears"
(not corn but a species of gray mullet
that has escaped my dictionary's net)
for half their asking price. The names of fish

XLVI

are always local, says the physicist
who summers here, untangling fishing lines
like mine, & whose tall stories show that even
science is personal. Claiming the latest
sub-atomic particle, epsilon,
originated in "Oops, Leon," he proves
the hit-or-miss nature of dismantling
matter among the theorists turning back
the clock to three minutes past the Big Bang,
which set the universe ticking down. I use
the same method in building my own world,
just as my ex-fighter-pilot neighbor
cobbles together a marble patio
in memory of his stone-mason father.

XLVII
Repairs gave new life to your kilim woven
in Mut, a town called by the alias
of the ancient earth goddess your name translates
as "with" & thus means "joyful." You always knew
that you would never live up to it, though,
till you became one with the earth, returned
to the roots your name has in an old word
for a grain measure, your mother's wish for you
come true the way the pattern in your weaving
appeared when the boy mending it withdrew
the olive thread that rounded out its design
from his Nike bag of hand-spun yarn dyed
every color. Unraveler of light,
he tied up loose ends to make you happy.

XLVIII
Turquoise fades from the sea & sky alike,
the sun paler than a Communion wafer.
A pleasure craft trailing a sprightly caique
scurries to dock before the light dies.
Kids gladly follow home the aroma
of steaming bulgur. A tortoise-shell tom
steals into some corn, waiting for the mice
that will show up at dark. A black goat
steps out of the shadow of an olive.
Flighty little nondescript birds get heard.
A cow lows to be milked, her calf kicking up
his heels. All flesh looks peachy at the last.
A girl fresh from the shower smells like rain.
Lightning in her eyes. Thunder in my heart.

XLIX
When I was thirty-something, I risked life
by smoking a bootblack's hash in Istanbul
& almost got greased by a chrome DeSoto,
walking under the influence. Five years
before, convinced a harmless-looking blue
Nova parked across Hope Street had my number,
I'd flushed my stash & switched to vitamins.
I "let it be," in the famous last words
of the Beatles. You had flown the first jumbo
jet here that summer for the operation.
Never again, I vowed, & would remember.
You came home, long hair cropped, & handed me
a marble egg I took to be a symbol
& brooded on until I hatched a life.

L
Twenty-plus years ago this Labor Day,
instead of flying back as I am now,
I stepped off Aegean Jet's night bus
&, touching down, first set foot in Izmir.
Seaside palms had cut their teeth on a sky
blue as September, & we'd reached the end
of a trip started on a Greyhound out
of the Twin Cities when I drummed my phone
number into my head, a souvenir
of childhood, & you murmured in the dark,
"I am a children." Your kid sister finding
her way through shade to where we'd come to light,
your mother waited in her stone-cool house,
your room the scene that night of our first time.

WISHFUL THINKING

1. MESSAGE IN A BOTTLE

We lose the light before it is too late
to see Labor Day's wispy new moon
curve into the ocean, an eyelash blond
as my appleseed-brown-eyed son's eyebrows
bleached by the sun as if caked with dried salt
one last time before he enters first grade
tomorrow. Summer's closed parenthesis,
the crescent moon lighting on the horizon
becomes a white sail bellied out by wind
& rides into the sunset even he
finds unnerving. I want to say to him:
We've all been there; the secret is to make
your way back here, where beach glass is as good
as currency, but able to read this.

2. ROUGH DRAFT

Holding his heart & seeing stars, my boy
stands behind bars as red as the fine lines
his class keeps inside to carve out small letters,
feet on the ground, & pledges his allegiance
to the flag without stumbling till he draws
a blank at *under God* (Ike's little add-on
in my day), *indivisible* proves a tongue-
twister, & *justice for all* gives him pause.
Word by brave word, the lump in my throat grows
as I remember coming to attention
every last morning ended with my marching
into school & signing up for the draft
the morning after I had turned eighteen,
putting my life on the line in no time.

3. AUTOBIOGRAPHY

When you write stories, it's okay to tell
what's happened in your life. My sentiments
exactly, except they're my first-grader son's
reason for not dreaming up aliens
for his illustrated narrative. Drawing
on the granddaddy of an octopus
he watched make short work of a crab last August,
he's represented it as also penning,
with one free arm & in the ink he saw
bled from it, a purple crayon likeness
of the blue Magic Marker original
it's eating. He figures life happens twice—
first out there & then in here, where it shows
its true colors once it's captured on paper.

4. S-CURVE

The clock in my Honda doesn't let my kid
circle back in time, its numbers composed
of lines straight as the roads that bore him always,
high-waisted jack pines waving on both sides.
Its stoplight-green read-out lacking in curves,
he rages in the back seat, at six partial
(like Navajos rounding off with white blankets
their foursquare red shoulders) to twists & turns
because the eye apes the pear-shaped blue planet
school has taught him is the apple of his.
Still, I see myself in him when he takes
the long way around again winding down
to the point of his short story, twisting words
& putting his heart in each turn of phrase.

ROCK COUNTRY

Oxford County, Maine

Here all the dead outnumber the living,
& what my father called a "marble orchard"
rises around each turn. Centuries past,
his people landed a stone's throw from where,
stop-sign red, my Cardinals cap guards against
far-from-distant shotguns aimed at small birds,
as I dream motherlodes of amethyst
or tourmaline but only strike fool's gold.

I've never looked his headstone in the face
whose rage for hunting had me popping off
in woods like these myself some forty years
ago this fall. I kneel with my own son
in quartz-cold air flecked with snow like mica,
digging for the stone with my name on it.

THE BOYS

Toward the end it got too dark to say
who was who in the father-&-son game
commemorating the last soccer season.
Play no sooner began than the pale sun
of November gave up the ghost, the earth
frozen the earliest in living memory.
By virtue of my age, I stood my ground
in goal, the final line of defense against

the kids. Shadows kicking the shins of shades-
to-be, they swarmed me in the gloom of dusk
& took their shots, my son for a hat trick.
Then time ran out, & with the other boys
he celebrated "killing the old guys."
Hearing about it all the long way home,
I hated thinking that someday we'd go
wordless into our separate nights, like men.

BLUE MONDAY

Rising to a dusk-gray day & the rain-
blackened limbs of my apple stripped bare

so disheartened me I barely had the heart
to raise my schoolboy from the depths of sleep,

but when I waited for the light to change,
hustling him off through Little Portugal,

I saw puddles like shards of mirrored windows
plywood had boarded up suddenly flash

azure, the street under my wheels now cobbled
with tiles the Portuguese named *azulejos.*

The sky had cleared a moment, & the water
had brought it down to earth, leaving me

an image I turned over in my mind
like the turquoise chip of sea glass from the Med

I worried in my pocket—the lucky charm
I'd found that could return me to the beach

even in winter, much as the aqua ink
slipping through my fingers while I write

takes me back to the source of never feeling
bored growing up an only child: those storms

that drove me inside out in the Midwest
sent me to the well of my own deep waters,

& when I got shipped off to class, I went
still dreamy on my dinghy-yellow bus.

PARENTAL GUIDANCE

1. MIRROR IMAGE

Shining my oxblood Dan Post's, I go back
to giving my salesman father's black oxfords
the sheen of the night sky all glossy with stars
Minnesota winters. I spared his arms
to save his heart when he had only reached
the age that I am now, & buffed his Florsheim's
the way my mother worked his brass-cold feet
to light a fire under his blood. As if
I rubbed a lamp to bring alive my genie,
my face slowly rose from each toe as dark
as every icehole that had swallowed it.
I didn't follow in his footsteps but schooled
myself in polishing these old black shoes
until I made out a face that could be his.

2. THE BOOKKEEPER

The beach at Blind Pass still as white as Liquid
Paper, an onionskin-thin paper fig
makes land unbroken, saying it's my day.
Some twenty years ago I didn't know
one shell from another till my twice-widowed
mother—the Gulf torn between blues then, too—
named every piece of luck the tide coughed up.
A decade later, time left her high
& dry the morning I found out my child
was swimming for this shore. At ten he hears
from me the names I learned from her at thirty
as now I seek my fortune in her memory,
my feet guided by her eye for what washed
up out of the depths to balance the books.

COUNTDOWN

As I collect my son from hide-&-seek,
asking him to call it a day & stop

blending with shadows as if going back
to where he hid out before he was born,

I could be standing on the shore & casting
lines into the blue in the hope a form

I know by heart will swim out of the dark
in silence, stealing "home" ahead of "It."

(Who'd choose to hang his head & count to ten
while everyone dissolves into the night?)

I tear my boy from play & march him off
toward the house & sleep—toward the time

that I won't see, I mean, when there will be
no one to find him or to walk him home.

DAYLIGHT SAVING

1

The first bees of the season buzz the snowdrops
hanging their heads & staring at their feet.
My father plants his foot in the springy earth
& throws out the season's first pitch, the ball
white as I remember the first snowfall.
His mitt, a Bill Doak model blackened by dirt
from the Thirties, fits him like a glove; mine's
too big for me. As much a ghost as him
in time, I see myself a memory
in my son's eyes as we play catch this morning
in our backyard, the new hardball his first.

2

I'm standing in my father's shoes, ten years
older than he was when he raked the earth
for Little League practice, my sneakers black
like his. After forty years he's still golden,
at home on the skinned infield the sun spotlights,
the center of a diamond-in-the-rough
as left & right he fungoes kids would-be
bleeders. Each grounder that he hits kicks up
the dust he'll be in ten years. The clock turned
forward last night, I'm stepping off baselines
five feet at a time for my son's first practice.

RETRIEVER

"I wish I had a dog to take me different
directions," my boy sighed as he trudged home
from school in his last week of being ten
& watched a headstrong golden drag its human
companion through the mud at the end of her rope.

Everybody is gone who always said
I'd no sooner learned to walk than I vanished
from Nana's picket-fenced backyard washday,
only to be spotted hours later climbing
Illion tied to the collar of her springer.

When I repeated his words, my son countered
they sounded like a song, as if he knew
he'd handed me a line I'd grab & let
lead me back through memory to retrieve time.

LATE RETURNS

1. First Morning in Asia Minor

Descended from the bus that fishtailed down
the coast all night, I couldn't swallow breakfast
(the driver bought; a tourist was a guest
back then). His runny fuchsia jam & stinking

white cheese added insult to near-injury,
after he'd already turned my stomach
with every last breathtaking chance he took
snaking through the dark above the Aegean.

First light showed me a landscape I'd first glimpsed
in my illustrated Bible at Sunday school,
but who knew I had found the promised land

of my own life, where I would taste the milk
& honey of the source, its salt & oil?
I hoped the food got better, that was all.

2. TOWARD AN ANNIVERSARY

Under the sun back at its height in June
a legless beggar spun round, dervish-wise,
frantic to catch the eye of each passerby
he made sidestep his limp, empty Levi's
twisted in Smyrna's cobblestoned agora
like Caesar's limbs contorted by a seizure.

Winding up a stairway that turned above
the swarm of streets into a honeycomb
of shops, I found a goldsmith in his cell
—behind locked doors & in the air-conditioned
isolation that glorifies the end
of this particular millennium—

& asked if he who could work miracles
would gild your hand-carved coral cameo
of Aphrodite in her bliss, a gift
commemorating ages spent intact.
Below, my guilt recalled, one still awaited
wild-eyed the miracle of some small change.

3. NEAR EAST SOLSTICE

Before farming became an industry
even here in the neighborhood of Eden,
watermelons never hit the stands
till the Fourth of July. Hence the kids' chant

I heard a woman laughingly recite
Father's Day at the beach as she dived in:
"Unless I find a watermelon rind
swimming in the sea, it's not warm enough

for me." Now the fruits of the earth obey
no timetable, all growing out of season,
so that it's every man for himself as far
as testing the waters. Seeing June again,

my father-in-law at seventy begged God
for one more year. Summer is paradise.

4. WESTERN EXPOSURE

Back on the cliffwalk to the Gulf of Chios
for a sunset swim, I fell in behind
three women wrapped from head to toe in patterns
of every color. Dressed as they believed
Allah desired, they felt their time had come,
the topless & us all-but-bottomless
gone now, our god brought low at last. Surprised
by me in my Speedo, they retraced their steps
in a hurry. Leaving, though, I passed the spot

where they had moved to get their feet wet, stockings
under shalvars beneath ankle-length skirts.
Two of them turned their backs, but the third raised
her open face to me as the sun went down.
Smiling, I wished her a timely *Good evening,*
& under the gold scarf concealing her hair
like a halo rubbed out at St. Sophia,
she flashed an olive-eyed smile in return,
as if we shared the same day in the sun.

5. SIGHTSEEING IN IZMIR

Like sparrows playing hit-&-run with crumbs
around a parkbench, two dark-haired sun-burnt
shoeshine-boy ragamuffins snatched in passing

half a Big Mac & a half-drunk Fanta
the woman in a denim skirt I'd stolen
peeks up had left behind at her outdoor

table. Their age, my son had seen nothing
as he dug, starving, into his gold nuggets,
his eye caught by the black-shrouded figure

seated nearby, her head under what looked
to be a hangman's hood with slits for seeing,
breathing, & inhaling fries & a shake.

The man with her undressed girls with his gaze,
& she missed nothing with her bird-quick glances.

6. Travelers' Advisory

"All days are beautiful," revealed our village
baker who daily turned white flour to gold
bagels with sesame seeds mechanically

hulled in America, "because they will
not come again," like the hibiscuses
—a.k.a. "Japanese roses" here—

that I'd seen flower fifty to a bush
at a time & then go limp, shriveled up
to nothing by sundown. Each morning after,

he asked if he was "good," but all I knew
was that he'd lived to see another day
June strawberries you'd melted down to jam

under the sun would ruby my plate drop
by drop, redder than ever now that August
brought out the light's dark side. One more summer

slowly bled to death the way my "heart,"
so called for lack of a better word, withered
under fire from you during each night's battle.

7. BESIDE THE HOLY CITY'S SACRED POOL

Once at Hierapolis, a booked-up ghost town
of a Roman necropolis with hot springs
where German little Caesars burn in sulfur,
a belly dancer neither young nor old
—castanets snapping like spun roulette wheels—
gyrated up to me all hips & lashes.

Forehead & upper lip sequined with sweat,
she whispered in the current lingua franca
the dirty word *money* & spoke her mind
in body language that said loud & clear,
My left cup runneth over with large bills,
in hopes that I, a tourist trapped, would get
the message I should pad her other breast
with wads of cash. I gave her all I had.

8. MINOR RUIN

Come summer, I would always stop to worship
at what's left of the temple Teos raised

to Dionysus. It's the way I paid
homage to his devotees, who loved too well

the spirit's blood—wine dark as Homer's sea
beyond the olives—& wowed small towns all

across Ionia with their song & dance.
Except their fellow citizens got sick

of how they acted while at home & banished
the whole gang to a village so remote

it doesn't have a name in history.
But when the Persians rode out of the east,

even the city fathers called it quits,
escaping into exile with the rest.

Abandoned to this day, the spot is best
remembered in the end as the birthplace

of the Greek poet Anacreon, who died
as he'd lived by choking on a grape seed.

9. SHELLS FROM OKINAWA IN THE AEGEAN

A friend of a friend passed them on to me
here below Troy from his Pacific island
I only knew from stories of its waters
my father told repeatedly to master
the Zero that burst into his stateroom
on his destroyer, where he'd stood his ground
on the bridge & made sure she'd stay afloat
before he felt the shrapnel riddling both

his legs. Their copper polished by the waves,
those shells the tide dredged up weren't salvaged live,
but they still spoke to me, because they called
back from deep time his words—one lucky warrior's
inventing history & a mythic age
as many years past now as I have seen.

10. HOME FROM IONIA

Another summer & its August sex
suddenly in the past, I caught myself

going downhill back in the land of autumn.
A lone copper beech leaf fell at my feet,

its downward spiral echoing the upward
swirl of smoke from my nightly barbecues

of coralfish, blackeyes, or Day-Glo orange
deep-water red mullets netted as far

below the Aegean as the smoke got off
the ground before always losing itself

in the Milky Way. Greasing my skids, acorns
oaks scattered like lost marbles in my path

set me up for a fall, but there green olives
still clung to my tree as a yellow jacket

with matching kneepads drilled for the oil in them
my neighbors' hands would harvest, distilling gold

from the sun the way I turn ancient history
here into the elixir of memory.